Princess in Prison
Freedom from Bondage

To Terrie
Live Free.
Blessings
Benford

By: Dannielle Benford

Preface

Why is it that little girls want to dress up

like a princess?

Who told her that's who she is?

"But ye are a chosen generation, a royal priesthood, a holy nation, a peculiar people; that ye should shew forth the praises of him who hath called you out of darkness into his marvelous light"

1 Peter 2:9 KJV

Preface

Princess in Prison was inspired through my testimony. This journey has not been an easy one, but one that need to be told. I received the release over 3 years ago to write my story, but it was hard. Perhaps, because I was not ready to release it. My prayer is that this book, my testimony, will encourage you to live free by letting go of past situations and circumstances which have kept you in bondage for so many years. The Bible tells us that we are royalty. No type of prison is fit for the daughter of the King. I present to you, Princess in Prison.

The glory of this latter house shall be greater than of the former, saith the Lord of hosts: and in this place will I give peace, saith the Lord of hosts.

Haggai 2:9 KJV

Scripture Quotation taken from the Holy Bible KJV/NIV and a definition used from Webster's Dictionary

ACKNOWLEDGEMENTS

To God be the Glory. I worship and adore you. To the all wise God, my Savior, my fortress, my refuge and the very breath that I breathe thank you for the strength to endure this path of life and thank you God, for always but always being right there.

Thank you Family. There are too many of you to name individually. Thank you to my mother Florine Benford. You have truly showed me what survival is. Thank you for being my mother. Thank you to my sister Florence Benford-Thompson, who has always been there for me never questioning my reasoning but always there. Thank you little big brother Edward Benford who has helped build and put together anything I ever needed for ministry never asking why. Sonia Hartman thank you for all that you do. To my best friends Yolanda Simmons, Pamela Olowu and Yvonca Medlock sometimes I feel like I would not have made it without you. Ingrid Benford-Watson thank you. To my aunts, whom I love and treasure; Aunt Georgia, Aunt Mary, Aunt Lizzie and Aunt Blanche, the pillars of our family, thank you.

A very special thanks to all those who have mentored me and who has spoken a word over my life and who allowed me to shadow them, never judging, but always a source of help: Evangelist Denise Jones, Prophetess Tracey Moore, and Vivian Renfro. Thank you, Pastor Gary M. Renfro for every talk, every lesson and the word of God that you spoke into my life.

To my Hebrew midwives:
Pastors Fred and Stephanie Timmons, thank you for receiving this broken vessel and pushing me to my destiny. Thank you to the entire Church of the Harvest family. I love every one of you.

Asia Benford, India Blake and Kendall Benford-Robinson, my children, thank you for never giving up on me as your mother and for trusting me to raise you and love you the only way I knew how. I love you with everything that is within me.

Thank you, Garrett Myers for creating this beautiful book cover.

Prayer

Dear Heavenly Father,
  Thank you for guiding me, strengthening me,
moving me and never leaving me during the
process. Thank you God for being my rock, my
wheel in the middle of the wheel, my food when
I am hungry, my water when I am thirsty.
Thank you for every time the devil thought he
had me, you blocked him. Father, I pray that
the souls who read this book will find comfort,
peace and refuge in You and will look to you in
times of trouble, at all times. Thank you God,
for loving me even when I did not love myself.
Thank you, God, for raising me up in your son
Jesus Christ's Holy Name. Amen!

Table of Contents

Introduction

About Princess in Prison

Scriptures and Confessions

Letters of Release

Daily Journal

Introduction

As a little girl I used to read about Princesses and I often wondered if one day I would become a princess like the ones I read about. I noticed that each Princess had her own battle, her own story and although it looked like she was losing the battle, she would always make a strong comeback.

Cinderella lost her parents and had to live with her mean step mother who only wanted the best for her own daughters and her two stepsisters who teased her put her down and used her as their personal maid. They made her feel worthless.

Then there was Snow White who because she was beautiful, she was hated by an evil queen who was full of rage and jealousy because she wanted her beauty. So, she tried to steal her destiny from her.

Anastasia, a young innocent princess who had nothing to do with the family decisions lost ten years of life due to memory loss running from the enemy who wanted to keep her from her destiny.

With each princess, there was always an enemy trying to keep the young princesses from her destiny. I was always told the enemy will try to stop you where you are, so he can keep you from reaching where you are going.

The Bible says, "The devil comes to steal, kill and destroy."

"The thief cometh not, but for to steal, and to kill, and to destroy: I am come that they might have life, and that they might have it more abundantly."

John 10:10 KJV

Princess in Prison

Chapter One
Princess in Prison

As a child, I remember being around family members all the time. At any given moment, we would have five or six different generations in our house and I loved it. I love family and family fun. I used to think that my family was the only family that got together all of the time, for every holiday and every birthday. We were a singing, card playing, domino slamming family and we were always together. So, if anything was going on in the family, we all knew about it.

When I was a little girl, Disney would play a movie every Sunday evening. I would get excited because I knew that I was going to see a princess that day. In every one of those movies, I saw a little bit of myself, but I always wondered where my happy ending was.

Cinderella got her prince, Sleeping Beauty woke up, Snow White was the fairest of them all, Belle married the Beast and Rapunzel finally got to let her hair down. Every one of them got their happy ending. I always wondered if I would have a happy ending too.

Each princess was in some type of bondage or there was always someone trying to destroy or kill them. I believe that even

1

though these are fairy tales, they all have some real-life truth in them.

Romans 8:17 says, "Now if we are children, then we are heirs-heirs of God and co-heirs with Christ, if indeed we share in his sufferings in order that we may also share in his glory." With that being said, we are royalty, which means that we are true Princes and Princess. At some point in our lives, we have all lived in a cage.

Sleeping Beauty was punished due to something that her parents did. I often wondered if the curse that was placed on my life was due to something that my mother and father did.

The history books say, if your mother and father are slaves when a child is born to them, then that child is born into slavery. I believe that my mother and father were in their own prison of lust and or love, which ever one you want to call it, I was a product of it. I believe, like Sleeping Beauty's story, my imprisonment started at my conception and had a lot to do with my mother and father's, let's just call it, "situation."

There were two main people in the Bible who were attacked before they were in the womb. Moses's death was ordered before he was even conceived, Jesus's death was ordered as well. So, it's safe to say that the devil already knows there is a call on your life and he is trying to stop you before you even come into the knowledge of knowing who you are.

When I was born, I didn't have a death threat on my life, but I was born with something wrong with my eyes. I was born with an eye condition called Amblyopia also known as lazy eye. This is a pretty common thing and can be corrected if the proper procedures are taken. I did have the surgery because my eyes were so bad that I could not see straight, clear or normal. After the surgery, the following steps that were required to correct the eye were not done properly. So, the sight in my right eye was damaged and I am now legally blind in my right eye.

The Enemy tried to take my sight at a very early age, but he knew that was not going to work. Now, seeing the call on my life, he knew that I would not need my eyes to do what God has called me to do.

After the failed attempt to correct my eye, I developed very low self-esteem. I felt ugly and lost, like I didn't belong, kind of like the ugly duckling did when he was born. He just did not fit in with the rest of his brothers and sisters.

Now, as I look back on all of that, I see why I never fit in. I was not supposed to. Pretty much most of my life, I felt like I did not fit in. My eyes were crossed and that made me different from all of the other kids. I was a target for someone to pick on, someone to bully and someone to hurt day after day. This was the start of my forty years of wandering in the wilderness. Although I was surrounded by family who loved me, I still felt lonely and unloved.

At a very early age, the invisible cage door was shut and locked. I had always felt like I was in a cage. Some will not understand what spiritual prison is, but this type of bondage is more powerful than being in a physical prison. The funny thing about this is that I lived in a prison that I did not even know existed. This prison that I was in was not made for a princess or royalty. So, I asked myself why was I in there. The only answer that I could come up with was that Satan himself tried to stop me at a very early age, before I could even begin.

Then, at the age of four, the prison door closed, and the chains were locked. Here is my story.

Chapter Two
The Beast

At age four, I found myself in a tale of Beauty and the Beast, although I never felt that I was beautiful. I used to watch that movie all the time and I felt like I was trapped, just like Belle. Belle was forced to be the prisoner of a beast and I was forced to live with a beast. The difference is Belle's beast loved her and treated her well. The things that the beast did to me, he had to hate me.

I can remember as far back as age four being visited by the beast in the middle of the night and the beast lying on top of me stealing from me: my breathe, my innocence, my purity, my virginity and my love. Yes, all that was stolen from me at a very young age. Imagine going through life with no love in you. So, not only did I have an eye disorder to live with, I had been violated in the worst way.

I never knew when he would come in the night, but I knew that he would come and tear into my little body, treating it like it was a grown woman's body. One night the beasts spoke and asked me if he could pee inside of me? Not knowing any better, I said yes, and my life was surely cursed at that point. Every time I think about it, I get weak. That is exactly what the enemy wanted, to keep me weak. After he urinated in me, he knew that there was no life in me. I was numb on the inside. I was numb on the outside. I was treated like a toilet. I looked up the definition of a toilet. Webster says that a toilet is a fixture in a room used for human urine and feces.

I cannot remember how long the beast came to visit me, but I do know that unlike Belle, I did not get a happy ending. Instead, I got a life of confusion and darkness. That night opened a portal of destruction for me. I was destroyed and contaminated. I thought that I was nothing and no one would ever want me. I was placed in bondage, in a captivity that would seem like a lifetime. I was a fixture in a room, used for human urine and feces and anything else they wanted to deposit into me. After that night, and as I got older, I always found myself in some type of ungodly sexual relationships. That is just the way it would be for the next thirty-five years or so.

One day at age ten, I was walking home from school with my cousins and somehow, we got separated. A boy not much older than me pulled a knife on me and made me follow him to the laundry mat located on the corner of Alexander and Twelfth Street. He made me go into the restroom with him and he raped me. How ironic that it happened in a restroom. He let me go and when I got home, I got a whopping because I came home late from school. I could not tell them why I was late because I was scared and ashamed.

The spirit of that beast just kept on following me and he would not leave me alone. After the rape, I knew then that I was used up and that no man would ever want me. So, I made it a point to never look a man in the eye. Every time a man would cross my path, I would hold my head down and look at the ground because I felt that I was not worthy enough to look him in the eye. I felt like I had the mark of the beast on my forehead and I felt that way for a very long time.

At age 16, I was introduced to a Spirit-filled, Word-based church. There, I learned so much about God and my Savior and I fell in love with the Word. This was a wonderful time in my life, but even with that, came destruction.

There was a man in the church that took me out for my 16th birthday. Before he took me home, he touched me in places that he should not have. I remember being so scared because he was a Caucasian man and I feared him.

I got away from him only to run into another Caucasian man in the church. He was even worse than the beast. His mother was my spiritual mentor. His mother and I were very close. She would pick me up and allow me to stay at her home every weekend. I so loved it because I knew that I would be able to go to church and get to sit in on women's Bible studies. I loved it, but it also came with a price.

Her son lived with her. He would come into my room and touch and feel on me, hoping that I would consent to what he was doing, but I never did.

One day, he tricked me and told me that we were going Christmas shopping to find a Bible for his mother. At that time, the only Christian bookstore in Austin was in south Austin. So, we headed to the bookstore, but when we got to South Congress, he detoured. We ended up under a bridge. I thought my life was over. I was very terrified of him. I just knew that he was going to kill me. Being under that bridge paralyzed me and I was frozen with fear. Then, he began to kiss me. I was weakened by fear. I really thought that he would kill me. Why would he take me under a bridge if he did not have plans to kill me? I thought it was a bad dream and that I would wake up from it, but it was real. I felt so dirty and violated.

After the kiss, something happened; something spooked him, and he got in a hurry to leave. I can only believe that in that moment, God saved me.

2 Thessalonians 3:3 says: "But the Lord is faithful, and he will strengthen you and protect you from the evil one".

I strongly believe that God was with me because after that, he never touched me again. I guess you can say I had an angel watching over me that day.

I was extremely damaged goods by the time I reached the age of eighteen. So I was able to give myself a way to whom I wanted to and because of my history anything went. It did not matter and why should it have mattered. After all, I was nothing more than a fixture in a room used for human feces and urine.

I will always remember the night that I was used as a toilet. Nobody knew I felt that way because I wore a mask. I wore that mask for the next twenty years.

I began to live a very promiscuous life. I was numb and had no life in me whatsoever. After all, I was only doing what was required of me. The only difference was that I was giving it away, so that they would not take it. I was helpless and did not know any better.

I often wonder if God heard my cry out to Him. I was so numb that I could not even feel hurt or pain. I felt like trash, for real and the only thing I could do was put on a mask an act like everything was okay. However; I was really a mess.

Later, in my early thirties, I was introduced to another beast. I mentioned earlier that the spirit of the beast followed me. This new thing was a drug, Ecstasy. I was so hooked on Ecstasy that I could not have sex without it, as if I was not already numb enough.

I had gotten to the point I did not want to feel anything, and I did not want to remember anything. Every time I had intercourse, it was a reminder of my little four-year-old body being treated like a grown woman. I was torturing myself and did not even realize it. Those pills made me feel like I was in control and that I could do whatever I wanted to do. Since I could no longer have sex without the pills, when I could not find that particular pill, I would buy some over the counter, sex enhancing pills. They did the job well.

Drinking wine and taking pills allowed me not to feel anything. So, when the rejection came, I did not feel that I was the one being rejected or, so I thought. When I was under the influence, I was able to be anyone that I wanted to be. I was able to fake myself into believing I was wanted and loved by those men. The reality of it all is that I was nothing to them but a good time for the moment. None of them ever made a commitment. I could never call any of them my man.

The pain was so bad that I started feeling it through the numbness. God can you hear me? The Bible says that God is with us at all times. I was not so sure about that. I suffered a great deal of pain and shame and I was alone suffering in silence.

Chapter 3
Suffering in Silence

If you were to ask anyone who knew me or was raised with me, none of them could tell you that I was ever sad, that I cried a lot or that I was always to myself. However; if they looked back at how I lived, they would probably be able to see depression written all over me. I was so depressed, but I always had a smile on my face, everything had to be positive and I always had to find the good in every situation. Truth be told, I was probably one of the saddest people in the world and although my mask covered it up, my actions showed differently.

There is no doubt that I was severely emotionally and physically traumatized as a little girl. I never received any help for it. I just had to simply live life like everything was peaches and cream. I lived everyday face to face with the beast, never able to confront it and it pained me to the point that I was very unstable.

Every family has that one who everyone thinks is crazy or should I say "special". I was that one. I often heard, "oh, she is crazy", "she is so unstable", "she is an idiot" or "she is just stupid". I used to scream out real loud in my head and I would say, "I am not Crazy!!!!!!!!!!! I am Hurt!!! I need help!!!" No one could hear me. I was not crazy, stupid or unstable. I was just simply hurt. I did not know how to live a normal life, so, I would run. But everywhere that I ran, my problems would run with me just as fast. I made bad decisions all the time, I just could not think. My heart was hurting. All I wanted was for someone to say, "Are you okay?" and stop saying, "Oh, Dannielle, she is just crazy".

When you hurt like that, yes, people will think you are crazy. Hurt people do crazy things. I could not share my pain because I wore a mask that said, I was fine, and that life could not be better. But, oh my God, I was dark on the inside, devastated and destroyed. I did not know how to say that I needed help because I was ashamed.

Shame caused me to miss out on a whole lot in life. It caused me: not be the mother that I needed to be to my children, not be the best employee on my past jobs, not be the best friend to my friends, not be a good daughter to my mother and it also caused me to not be good to myself. I did not know how to let someone know that I was depressed and ashamed of it. Instead, I wore a mask. So many looked up to me and I could not let them down. I had to continue with my act and never get help for the pain that I felt.

I was very depressed for so long that I had forgotten what it was like to live a happy, unmasked life. Shame caused me to be disappointed in myself. I suffered a long, long, long time. As I look back on it, I cannot believe how dark I was. I pretended to be in the light, but my light was dull. No, my light had burnt out. I lived a very hurt life and I did not know how to communicate that and it cost me so much.

In the book of Samuel, the Word says, that "after Tamar's brother raped her, she went to live with another brother and she lived a desolate life." Can you imagine that? That was me: empty trying to pretend to be full, dark but trying to imitate light, frightened but trying to live brave, very ugly but trying to live pretty, I was lost and did not want to be found.

Suffering in silence is a tool of the enemy and it took me a very long time to understand that. I understand it now. I just recently realized that I suffered in silence and basically my life was a life lived behind a mask.

In 2nd Samuel chapter 13, it describes the rape of Tamar, daughter of King David. Tamar was a beautiful woman and her brother Amnon became obsessed with her. He got her alone, raped her and then abandoned her. After he raped her, Amnon hated her and he would not marry her. Her father did not do anything about it. No one in my life did anything about it!!!!!!!! Can you imagine something like this happening and you had to live like Tamar? Well, that is pretty much how I felt for forty years, Raped and Abandoned……..

I did not let anyone know that the molestation, the rape and the ungodly sexual relationships made me feel less than zero because I was ashamed.

The Word says in 1 Corinthians 13:10, "There hath no temptation taken you but such as is common to man: but God is faithful, who will not suffer you to be tempted above that ye are able; but will with the temptation also make a way to escape, that ye may be able to bear it." I love this scripture and its truth. If it was not true, I would not be here today. God provided a way of escape.

Prayer

Daddy God, Abba Father, thank You for showing me the way and for being the way. In Your Word, it says that you are Emmanuel and that You are with us. Thank You, God, for keeping me when I did not want to be kept. Thank you, Lord, for removing the pain and the shame. Thank You for being the One who lit my light and brought me back to life. You are my Protector and I see now that you had a hedge of protection over my life for such a time as this. Thank you, God, for knowing the plan that you have me and giving me beauty for my ashes. God, thank You for loving me enough and pulling me out of a horrible pit, just like you did for David. God, I thank You in Jesus' name, Amen!!!!

Chapter 4
The Journey

As I look back over my life, I can truly say that this Journey has been one of ups and downs, joy and pain, sun and rain. It has been a journey of giving up and letting go and a journey of I do not want to be here anymore that changed to I want live forever.

If I had to do it all over again, I would do it the same way. There is purpose and meaning to everything in life. In other words, there was reason for my journey.

If I had to pick a title for my life it would be, "What now?" It seemed like there was always something. First, an eye disability, then molestation, to rape, to fondling, to abortion, to promiscuity. There were two divorces, to having three children by three different men, to living a lie. I could go on and on, but I will not.

So, you ask, where God was in all this. I used to wonder that as well. As a matter of fact, I wondered that my whole life until I came to know Him as my Lord and Savior, but we will talk about that in another chapter.

The path that I chose to take in life, I chose because of what happened to me. I blamed someone else for a very long time in my journey. I blamed the beast for all my bad decisions, for all my mistakes and for all my mess ups.

That path of Promiscuity became a wide-open path. I totally blamed this on the beast. He left his spirit in me and I did not know how to cast it out. So, it became me. Nothing about what I was doing or who I was doing it with felt wrong. It felt right because that is all I knew. The men were everywhere, and no one turned me down. I was in my element, my zone. This was something I was good at. The sad thing about this part of my life is that it was actually worse than being molested because I was giving myself away like it was nothing. I found myself in hotels, in homes or apartments of men that I did not know and not even knowing their names. That is what I became and saving myself meant nothing. I mean, why? When that beast urinated in me, it left me numb to life. The reason why it was so easy to be with those men was because I felt nothing. I was still. I was in a very dark place in life and no one knew it because of the act. I hated myself. I hated the way I looked, and I hated the way men looked at me. Hence, the reason why even today, it is hard to hear the words, "you are a beautiful woman". How could I be beautiful? Someone used me as a toilet. Selah. A toilet is not beautiful, it is not even pretty. As I am writing this, tears are streaming down my face because I am finally free from my past and I now know who I am and my value and my worth and why God kept me.

The scripture says in Revelations 12:10-12, "And I heard a loud voice saying in heaven, Now is come salvation, and strength, and the kingdom of our God, and the power of his Christ: for the accuser of our brethren is cast down, which accused them before our God day and night. And they overcame him by the blood of the Lamb, and by the word of their testimony; and they loved not their lives unto the death. Therefore rejoice, ye heavens, and ye that dwell in them. Woe to the inhibiters of the earth and of the sea! for the devil is come down unto you, having great wrath, because he knoweth that he hath but a short time."

I have overcome, and the accuser is cast down.

For such a Time as This

"And I thank Christ Jesus our Lord, who hath enabled me, for that he counted me faithful, putting me into the ministry;"

1 Timothy 1:12 KJV

For such a Time as This

For if thou altogether holdest thy peace at this time, then shall there enlargement and deliverance arise to the Jews from another place; but thou and thy father's house shall be destroyed; and who knoweth whether thou art come to the kingdom for such a time as this?

Esther 4:14 KJV

Chapter 5
For Such a Time as This

I now understand that my journey was meant to be. I understand it to be warfare. Although at the time, I did not have a clue. I just thought that it was my plot in life and that is just what it was. I know now that the enemy was trying his best to destroy me, so that I would not be a mouth piece for the Lord for such a time as this.

For a very long time, I was a mess and could not tell my story to anyone or if I did, I told it like it did not affect me, when all along it ripped me in to pieces. It separated me from reality. I never wanted to share my story because no one ever saw me as a negative person and I felt that if I started talking about what happened to me that would be how people would see me, "negatively". So, I did not talk about my past openly. However, I did tell a few people here and there.

In December 2013, at the Broken Pieces conference, I was delivered from the shame and embarrassment of being molested and raped. I was able to actually deal with it and I began to tell people my story. In January 2014, the Lord released me to tell my testimony to five people through an email. After I released my testimony in that email, the phone calls and emails came and each person that was on the email responded, two of them releasing their own testimonies, so I knew at that time, that it was now, "For such a time as this".

Like Esther, who broke her silence so that her people could be free, in the book of Esther chapter 4:14, I too broke my silence. If I would have kept quiet, perhaps those two ladies would not be free today. A few months after I released my testimony, one of the young ladies who lived in another city asked if I could come and speak and give my testimony. With the Lord's and my Pastor's permission, I went to speak and gave my testimony. There was one young lady there that I connected with so deeply in the Spirit that I began to prophesy over her. The Lord spoke through me to her. I remember several conversations with her after the speaking engagement. She became free and began to forgive people so that she could stay free.

Several months after that, I gave my first healing and deliverance conference; I remember how liberty reigned in the atmosphere which we were in. For such a time as this was happening right before my very eyes. I began to understand the why behind my past. It was bigger than me and it was not about me.

A month after the conference, I was asked to give my testimony and several women came to me after that conference letting me know their stories and that they had not ever told anyone. Those women were freed, and each one said that they were going to begin telling their stories, so that others could hear and become free from their bondage.

According to scripture, if Esther had kept quiet, then she and her father's house would have perished. Relief and deliverance would have come from another place. I will tell my testimony quite often now because I understand that I went through it for such a time as this. I am called for such a time as this!!! If I decide not to give my testimony, God will always have a ram in the bush.

Chapter 6
The Call

Have you ever noticed that most people who are called by God have a great testimony? I mean, they have gone through in some type of way. When I read about some of the people in the Bible, I looked at their stories and boy did they go through some things. Look at Moses. He murdered a man and still carried out his calling. Jonah ran and was swallowed up by a great fish, but he repented and walked out his calling. Elijah hid in a cave, but he came out and faced his fears and finished what he was called to do. Paul did a lot of bad things to Christians and he even changed and walked in his calling. So, it is safe to say that everything I went through and experienced, it was equipping me for the calling on my life.

When I was going through, I was thinking of everything but that this might be a call by God. It was the furthest thing from my mind. As a matter of fact I was feeling like I had been punished by God. I remember saying why would God use someone like me? But now, I ask, why would He not use someone like me: someone that has been through, someone who seemed unstable, someone who could not make up her mind someone who was in bondage for forty years?

Forty is the number of testing. The Israelites were in the wilderness for forty years and when they come out, some of them were used to help get God's people to the Promise Land. I passed the test. I did not die in the process, meaning I did not give up; I did not throw in the towel. I repented and went on to Nineveh.

The scripture that speaks to me,

"And I thank Christ Jesus our Lord, who hath enabled me, for that he counted me faithful, putting me into the ministry;"

1 Timothy 1:12 KJV

Although I wanted to give up, oh, so many times, I could not because like Jeremiah, it was like fire shut up in my bones and I was called before I was in my mother womb. I must follow Jesus as my Lord and savior. I said in an earlier chapter, that I would share Jesus as my Lord and Savior. I asked the questions earlier: "Where was God in all my suffering? Why did He allow all those horrific things to happen?" Well, in the book of Job, God said to Satan, "have you considered my servant Job?" I just replaced my name with Job, "Have you considered my servant Dannielle?"

God allowed some things to happen in my life, but through it all, He kept me. The beast could not kill me and it was all for such a time as this. There were times when Job wanted to give up and throw in the towel. Job was so done he wished the day he was born had never happened, but he stood the test, got the victory and God received the glory.

As I looked at Job's story, it was a little different than what we go through. I stated in an earlier chapter that if I had to title my life it would have been "What Now?". Job lost everything in one day, in a matter of minutes. He did not have time to say, "what now" all he could do was tear his clothes and mourn. The one thing I learned from Job is that if we lose everything, but still have Jesus, we have more than enough and can start over. God never took his hedge off Job. He kept him through it all. I believe in God and I believe God. He will never leave nor forsake us. Knowing this, I answered the call to ministry.

Chapter 7
Here Am I

I answered the call to ministry in May of 2014 and was ordained January 2017, under the leadership of Pastors Fred and Stephanie Timmons. I knew at a very early age that I would be in ministry, not only was it prophesied, but I have always felt connected. I remember my friends calling me "holy roller" at a young age. I was able to interpret dreams and my friends did not like that or that I knew things that were going to happen, before it happened. These were and are signs that my life was more than me being a toilet, a fixture in a room used for human urine and feces or being some man's treat for the night. I should have known when I stood out in that school yard and everyone picked on me because my eyes were crossed that my life would be sold out for Christ.

With that being said, it does not mean that I will now walk through life and everything is cupcakes and butterflies. As a matter of fact, in 2 Timothy 2:12, the Word says,

"If we suffer, we shall also reign with him: if deny him, he also will deny us."

I said earlier, that I chose the path that I did because of what happened to me. Now, I choose the path that I live because of what happened to HIM. He died on the cross for me and because He did I have received salvation. I am healed through His stripes and I am delivered through His blood. He loves me and because of that I can live clean. I live a celibate life and I enjoy this new path that I am on. He carried me then and He carries me now. Now, I must walk out my assignment and know that I can do all through Christ things that strengthen me. (Philippians 4:13)

Accepting the call means sacrifice, its means giving up and letting go of a lot of things. It means being separated and sometimes spending seasons alone and a lot times, people will not understand. Sometimes, separation is necessary in order to hear the voice of God. Abraham was called to leave his family, Moses was sent to the backside of the desert. Both of these men were mighty servants of God, but they had to be raised up, tested and tried. Go back and read their stories and you will see what I am talking about.

When I said "yes", I said yes to His will, to His way and to His work. It does not matter who it separates me from or who it identifies me with. It was God who saved me and pulled me out of a horrible pit and I will serve Him for the rest of my days. I was a Princess in Prison and now I am a servant of the Lord God Almighty and I am free. The Word says, "that who the Son sets free is free indeed." (John 8:36) To God be the Glory!!!!!!

Beauty for Ashes

Father, I thank you for my life, the good, the bad and the ugly. I thank you for the ups and the downs. I thank you for the valleys and the mountains. Thank you for being with me through it all. Thank you, God for never leaving me nor forsaking me. Thank you for bringing me through the valley and pulling me up out of a horrible pit and for keeping in times when I did not want to be kept. Thank you, God for you are the author and finisher of my faith, the beginning and the end, the alpha and the omega and everything in between. Lord, I love you. I am nothing without you. You said in Your Word Isaiah 61:3:

"To appoint unto them that mourn in Zion, to give unto them beauty for ashes, the oil of joy for mourning, the garment of praise for the spirit of heaviness; that they might be called trees of righteousness, the planting of the Lord, that He might be gloried." Thank you, God for beauty for ashes. Thank you for beauty for ashes, Thank you God for beauty for ashes and a garment of Praise for my heaviness. Create in me God, a clean heart and renew in me a right spirit. My life is not my own, to you I belong, in Jesus Name, Amen and Amen.

About Princess in Prison

Princess in Prison was birthed in 2014 and was my assignment. I am to go out and help women and young ladies to come out of the prison which they have put themselves in, to help them realize that the door to the prison is not locked and through Christ Jesus we can escape and be healed and delivered.

Princess in Prison is my testimony. My prayer is that it will help deliver women all over the world. I was in bondage, captivity and prison but I no longer claim that. I have confronted and conquered my past. I am no longer in a sex driven prison. I am not a slave to men. I am no longer walking in self-pity. I am no longer angry, mad or bitter. I am free. I am no longer afraid to look a man in the eye. I am no longer afraid to receive the compliment that I am beautiful. I no longer cry myself to sleep and wish that I was no longer here. Why? Because I served my time bound up in the generational curse and I have renounced that it all be dismissed, demolished and destroyed and that it shall not return to me or to the generations after me. The curse is reversed in Jesus' Name, Amen and Amen!!!!!

Prison is no place for a princess. I encourage you to straighten up your crown, repent and move forward. We do not have but a few days left here on earth and I will rejoice and be glad in it and live a life of peace, joy and happiness. I didn't know who I was as a child or as a young woman, but God.

I went to a conference in 2010, it was themed, "The Princess Within" and that is when I found out that I was a princess, and that I was royalty, that I am the daughter of the King. After that conference, no one could tell me I was not a Princess or that I was not the daughter of the King. I realized who and whose I was at that point. It was the best feeling ever. Since then, I can very strongly announce who I am. It was not long after that, everything that was stolen from at age four was restored: my love, my peace, my joy, my happiness, my purity and my beauty.

Through all of this, I have learned that forgiveness is freedom.

"And when ye stand praying, forgive, if ye have ought against any: that your Father also which is in heaven may forgive you your trespasses."

Mark 11:25 (KJV)

I knew that it was not you.

"For we wrestle not against flesh and blood, but against principalities, against powers, against the rulers of the darkness of this world, against spiritual wickedness in high places"

Ephesians 6:12 KJV

Dear Beast,

I forgive you.

I know it's been a very long time since you have visited me. I am older now and I am stronger. I am writing this letter to tell you that I forgive you and I pray that you are well and released from the bondage and prison which you have been in. I understand that it was not you who hurt me, according to Ephesian 6:12. I did not know that back then and I hated you, but because I have been freed and saved, I can release you from this terrible thing that has happened. I love you and may God bless you.

Blessings,
The Princess

Scriptures and Confessions

I can do all things through Christ who strengthen me. (Philippians 4:13) I am strong in the Lord and there is nothing that I cannot overcome or conquer for His Word says in Roman 8:37 NIV, "No, in all these things we are more than conquerors through him who loved us." So, I call everything forth that I lost and that I shall have in Jesus' Name.

I plead the canopy of protection, Psalms 91:11 KJV over my life. "For he shall give his angels charge over me and keep thee in all thy ways."

Scriptures that helped me along the way:

Have not I commanded thee? "Be strong and of a good courage; be not afraid, neither be thou dismayed: for the Lord thy God is with thee whithersoever thou goest."

Joshua 1:9 KJV

"Casting all your care upon him; for he careth for you."

1 Peter 5:7 KJV

"To appoint unto them that mourn in Zion, to give unto them beauty for ashes, the oil of joy for mourning, the garment of praise for the spirit of heaviness; that they might be called trees of righteousness, the planting of the Lord, that he might be glorified."

Isaiah 61:3 KJV
"But they that wait upon the Lord shall renew their strength; they shall mount up with wings as eagles; they shall run, and not be weary; and they shall walk, and not faint."

Isaiah 40:31 KJV

"When thou passest through the waters, I will be with thee; and through the rivers, they shall not overflow thee: when thou walkest through the fire, thou shalt not be burned; neither shall the flame kindle upon thee."

Isaiah 43:2 KJV

"For I know the thoughts that I think toward you, saith the Lord, thoughts of peace, and not of evil, to give you an expected end."

Jeremiah 29:11 KJV

My Favorite
Scriptures

"I will praise thee; for I am fearfully and wonderfully made: marvelous are thy works; and that my soul knoweth right well."

Psalms 139:14 KJV

"And be not conformed to this world: but be ye transformed by the renewing of your mind, that ye may prove what is that good, and acceptable, and perfect, will of God."

Romans 12:2 KJV

Royalty
Who I Am

"But ye are a chosen generation, a royal priesthood, a holy nation, a peculiar people; that ye should shew forth the praises of him who hath called you out of darkness into his marvelous light:"

1 Peter 2:9 KJV

About the Author

I was born on October 29th, 1969 and raised in Austin, Texas. As a child, she attended Church of the Living God, under the leadership of her Uncle, the late Reverend R.H. Hawkins. This is where it all began, and the foundation was laid.

I became a member of Church of the Harvest, in November 2014, under the leadership of Pastors Fred and Stephanie Timmons. I am a servant first. Wherever there is a need, she will serve. I graduated from the Sonship School of the First Born in 2015 and was ordained a Minister in January 2017. I currently serves as a Minister, Children's Church Ministry leader and on the Evangelism team. I do what I do because I love the Lord.

I have three beautiful children: Asia, India and Kendall, and a Precious granddaughter, Paris. They keep me going and I love them deeply.

I am the Founder of L.A.D.I.E.S (waiting on the promises of God), a ministry that is destined to go out unto the nations to give my testimony, to teach and preach the gospel to women all over the world, so that healing and deliverance can take place and souls can be saved through the words of our Lord and Savior.

My mission is to walk the walk and talk the talk of my Lord and Savior. My prayer is that many will be made free through my testimony and my obedience to God, by going out and ministering the word of God. Send me Lord I will go.

Forgiveness freed me, and my prayer is that reading my testimony will help you to forgive those that hurt you and understand that forgiveness will bring peace to you. Do not allow unforgiveness to keep you in a dark place. We have work to do, but we will not be able to move forward until we are able to forgive. Tomorrow is not promised, so let's get it done today.

Forgiveness

I Forgive You

"And when ye stand praying, forgive, if ye have ought against any: that your Father also which is in heaven may forgive you your trespasses.   But if ye do not forgive, neither will your Father which is in heaven forgive your trespasses."

Mark 11:25-26 KJV

I forgive you

Letters of Release

"Clothe yourselves with compassion,
kindness, humility, gentleness and patience.
Bear with each other and forgive whatever
grievances you may have against one another.
Forgive as the Lord forgave you."

Colossians 3:12-13 KJV

Dear _____, I forgive you.

_____

_____

_____

_____

_____

_____

_____

_____

_____

_____

_____

_____

_____

_____

_____

_____

_____

_____

_____

_____

_____

_____

_____

Dear _____, I forgive you.

_____

_____

_____

_____

_____

_____

_____

_____

_____

_____

_____

_____

_____

_____

_____

_____

_____

_____

_____

_____

Dear _____, I forgive you.

_____
_____
_____
_____
_____
_____
_____
_____
_____
_____
_____
_____
_____
_____
_____
_____
_____
_____
_____
_____
_____
_____
_____
_____
_____

Dear _____, I forgive you.

_____
_____
_____
_____
_____
_____
_____
_____
_____
_____
_____
_____
_____
_____
_____
_____
_____
_____
_____
_____
_____
_____
_____

Dear _____, I forgive you.

_____

_____

_____

_____

_____

_____

_____

_____

_____

_____

_____

_____

_____

_____

_____

_____

_____

_____

_____

_____

_____

_____

Dear _____, I forgive you.

_____

_____

_____

_____

_____

_____

_____

_____

_____

_____

_____

_____

_____

_____

_____

_____

_____

_____

_____

_____

_____

_____

_____

Dear _____, I forgive you.

_____
_____
_____
_____
_____
_____
_____
_____
_____
_____
_____
_____
_____
_____
_____
_____
_____
_____
_____
_____
_____
_____
_____
_____
_____

Dear _____, I forgive you.

_____
_____
_____
_____
_____
_____
_____
_____
_____
_____
_____
_____
_____
_____
_____
_____
_____
_____
_____
_____
_____
_____
_____
_____

Dear _____, I forgive you.

_____

_____

_____

_____

_____

_____

_____

_____

_____

_____

_____

_____

_____

_____

_____

_____

_____

_____

_____

_____

_____

_____

_____

_____

Dear _____, I forgive you.

_____

_____

_____

_____

_____

_____

_____

_____

_____

_____

_____

_____

_____

_____

_____

_____

_____

_____

_____

_____

_____

_____

_____

_____

Dear Reader,

I pray that my testimony has helped in your own situation and has encouraged you to do better, to forgive and move forward. God's plan for you is far greater than you can ever imagine. Take life one day at one and never take matters into your own hands.

The Bible is our road map to the life. I believe there is something in the Bible for every situation. God said, that He will not put more on us that we can bear. He will provide a way of escape. There is no way a four-year-old can handle what happened to me. So, I know that God was with me and that He kept me.

Do not give up. Allow God to show you His plan that He has for you. Pray without ceasing. Ask and you shall receive. Stay connected to the vine and you will always be loved and taken care of. Remember, there is nothing too hard for God. Peace be with you. Take some time to write out your journey. Journaling is therapy.

Daily Journal

Day 1

Dear Lord, today is _____,

Day 2

Dear Lord, today is _____,

Day 3

Dear Lord, today is _____,

Day 4

Dear Lord, today is _____,

Day 5

Dear Lord, today is _____,

Day 6

Dear Lord, today is _____,

Day 7

Dear Lord, today is _____,

Day 8

Dear Lord, today is _____,

Day 9

Dear Lord, today is _____,

Day 10

Dear Lord, today is _____,

Made in the USA
San Bernardino, CA
12 January 2018